The Care & Keeping of YOU Journal

illustrated by Norm Bendell

★ American Girl®

D0150839

Published by American Girl Publishing, Inc.

Copyright © 2001, 2008 by American Girl, LLC

Questions or comments? Call 1-800-845-0005,
visit our Web site at **americangirl.com**,
or write to Customer Service, American Girl,
8400 Fairway Place, Middleton, WI 53562-0497.

Printed in China

09 10 11 12 13 LEO 10 9 8 7 6

All American Girl marks are trademarks of
American Girl, LLC.

Editorial Development: Elizabeth A. Chobanian,
Michelle Watkins, Therese Kauchak Maring

Art Direction & Design: Chris Lorette David

Production: Janette Sowinski, Lori Armstrong,
Jeannette Bailey, Kendra Schluter, Lisa Bunescu,
Judith Lary

Illustrations: Norm Bendell

Medical Consultant: Dr. Lia Gaggino, Pediatrician

This book is not intended to replace the advice of
or treatment by physicians, psychologists, or other
health-care professionals. It should be considered
an additional resource only. Questions and concerns
about mental or physical health should always be
discussed with a doctor or other health-care provider.

Dear Reader,

If it hasn't already, your body is about to go through some big changes. Along with these changes come lots of different emotions. Truth is, growing up isn't easy. But you can take control by taking care of yourself—inside and out.

This companion journal to the book *The Care and Keeping of You* is filled with ideas to get you started. From checklists and quizzes to fill-in-the-blanks, doodles, and daydreams, all you need is a pencil and a private place. Fill it in. Check it off. And learn about yourself!

Just remember there's more to you than just your body—there's your mind, your heart, and your spirit, too. And all these parts of you add up to someone wonderful.

Your friends at *American Girl*

About Me

You are more than just the reflection you see in the mirror. Your **mind, body,** and **spirit** make you unique.

Mind

My favorite subject in school is

I'm fascinated by

I want to learn more about

I love to read

I love to write

Body

Age: ....

Height: ....

I'm ☐ left-handed ☐ right-handed

Spirit

Time of day I'm at my best: ....

People I love: ....

....

Things that make me happy: ....

Things that make me sad: ....

Best friends: ....

....

Things I wish I could change about the world: ....

....

....

Who Am I Like?

No one will ever be exactly like you. But chances are **you see similarities** between yourself and your parents or relatives. How are you like another member of your family?

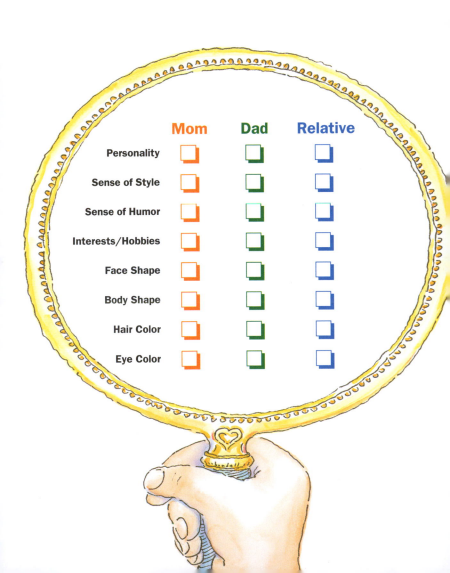

	Mom	Dad	Relative
Personality	☐	☐	☐
Sense of Style	☐	☐	☐
Sense of Humor	☐	☐	☐
Interests/Hobbies	☐	☐	☐
Face Shape	☐	☐	☐
Body Shape	☐	☐	☐
Hair Color	☐	☐	☐
Eye Color	☐	☐	☐

Inside and out, here's what makes me uniquely me:

....

....

....

....

....

....

....

....

....

....

....

....

....

....

I Am . . .

Circle the words that best **describe you.**

Caring

Thoughtful

Giggly

Clever

Serious

Funny

Kind

Outrageous

Dedicated

Musical

Honest

Happy

Quiet

Clumsy

Artistic

Smart

Athletic

Verbal

Goofy

Loyal

Sensitive

Hard-working

Informed

Creative

Colorful

Assertive

Sincere

Affectionate

Warm

Lazy

physical

Shy

Compassionate

Silly

Studious

Fearful

Courteous

polite

Friendly

Energetic

Bold

Moody

Independent

Logical

Messy

Loving

Easy-going

Loud

Irritable

Stylish

Proud

Gentle

Top three words I would use
to describe me:

Carefree

1. ....

2. ....

Theatrical

3. ....

Here's Why!

How do the words you chose on the previous page match how you **think, act,** or **feel?**

Word **1.** .... describes me because ....

....

....

....

....

....

....

....

....

....

....

Word **2.** .... describes me because ....

....

....

....

....

....

....

....

Word **3.** .... describes me because ....

....

....

....

....

....

....

Style File

Everyone has her own **special style.** What's yours?
Fill these pages with clippings, photos, and doodles of
things that say *you*.

Making the Grade

As you get older, the list of things you can do gets longer. Think of this as your own personal **report card**—a tally of all the things you're **good at,** as well as the skills you'd like to **improve.**

	I'm awesome at	I'm good at	I'm O.K. at	I wish I were better at
Math	☐	☐	☐	☐
English	☐	☐	☐	☐
Science	☐	☐	☐	☐
Social Studies	☐	☐	☐	☐
Music	☐	☐	☐	☐
Art	☐	☐	☐	☐
Sports	☐	☐	☐	☐

	I'm awesome at	I'm good at	I'm O.K. at	I wish I were better at
Listening	☐	☐	☐	☐
Sharing	☐	☐	☐	☐
Positive Thinking	☐	☐	☐	☐
Organizing	☐	☐	☐	☐
Communicating	☐	☐	☐	☐

Three other things I'm awesome at:

1. ....

2. ....

3. ....

Goal-Getter

Take one thing you wish you were better at and **set a specific goal.**

I wish I were better at ....

....

My specific goal is to ....

....

Who can help me and how they can help: ....

....

....

....

Three things I'll do to achieve my goal:

1.

2.

3.

Roadblocks and how I'll get past them:

How long and how often I'll work on my goal:

Changes

You're going through some **pretty big changes**—inside and out. Think about how you were a year ago versus how you are today. Write about the changes that have taken place:

At school: ....

....

At home: ....

....

To my body: ....

....

In my friendships: ....

....

....

In my interests: ....

....

....

....

How these changes make me feel:

Changes I'm waiting for:

Taking Care of Myself

Take **control** of your growing body by taking care of it. Now it's more important than ever, while you're going through **big changes.** It may feel like there's a lot to **remember,** but the following lists will help you break it down. Check off the things you already do.

Every Day

- ☐ Wash my face (morning and night) with mild soap and warm water

- ☐ Brush, floss, and rinse my teeth (in the morning, at night, and after eating)

- ☐ Brush my tongue

- ☐ Shower or bathe

- ☐ Apply deodorant

- ☐ Clean my newly pierced earlobes (three times a day with a cleanser recommended by the technician)

- ☐ Wash my hands after I use the bathroom and before I eat

- ☐ Comb or brush my hair

- ☐ Get at least eight hours of sleep

- ☐ Clean my contacts or eyeglasses

- ☐ Drink six to eight glasses of water

At Least Weekly

❑ Wash my hair (several times a week)

❑ Wash my hairbrushes and combs

❑ Exercise enough to get sweaty
(three times a week for at least
20 minutes each time)

❑ Trim my nails

Once or Twice a Year

❑ See the doctor for a physical exam (once a year)

❑ See the dentist for a dental exam (twice a year)

❑ See the eye doctor for an eye exam
(once a year)

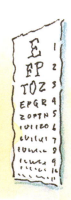

Here are some other things I do to take care of myself:

_____

_____

_____

_____

_____

_____

_____

_____

_____

_____

_____

_____

Bubble Trouble

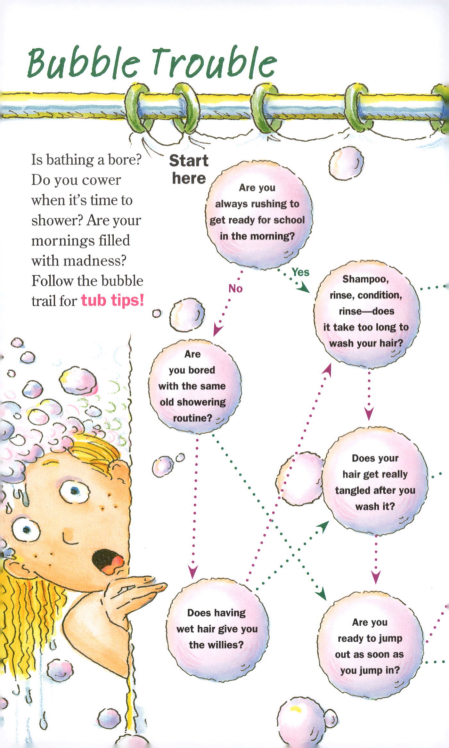

Is bathing a bore? Do you cower when it's time to shower? Are your mornings filled with madness? Follow the bubble trail for **tub tips!**

Start here

Are you always rushing to get ready for school in the morning?

No

Yes

Shampoo, rinse, condition, rinse—does it take too long to wash your hair?

Are you bored with the same old showering routine?

Does your hair get really tangled after you wash it?

Does having wet hair give you the willies?

Are you ready to jump out as soon as you jump in?

Do you wish there was a speedier way to get clean?

Timely Tips

It sounds like you need to save time in the shower. Try showering at night instead of in the morning, and you won't feel so rushed before school. Use a shampoo/conditioner combo to save time. And don't use too much. A small squirt is all you need, and it will rinse out faster than a handful.

Is taking care of your hair a hassle?

Hair Scare

All tangled up? Here are a few tips for easier hair care. Don't rub your hair dry with a towel. Instead, pat it—it won't get as tangled. And keep in mind, the shorter your hair is, the less time it'll take to dry. No matter what length your hair is, make sure you get it trimmed regularly to help prevent tangles.

Do you just want showering to be more fun?

Shower Power

If showering is a snore, it's time for a new routine. If you've been using the same bath products for a long time, try a new brand of soap or shampoo. A fresh scent will perk you up! Trade in your washcloth for a cute sponge. And sing your favorite tunes while you shower—your voice will sound great!

Pampering Myself

Top ten ways to boost your **mind, body,** and **spirit:**

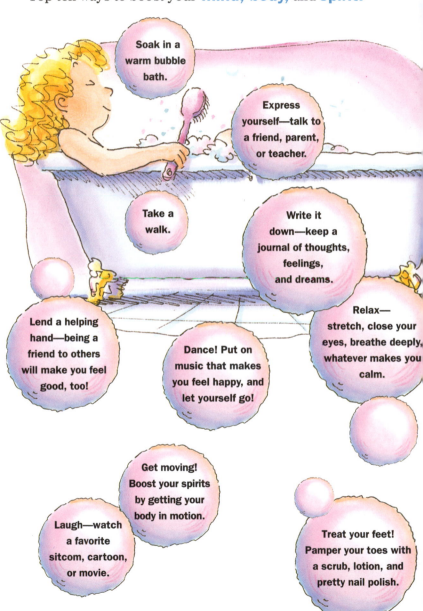

Soak in a warm bubble bath.

Express yourself—talk to a friend, parent, or teacher.

Take a walk.

Write it down—keep a journal of thoughts, feelings, and dreams.

Lend a helping hand—being a friend to others will make you feel good, too!

Dance! Put on music that makes you feel happy, and let yourself go!

Relax—stretch, close your eyes, breathe deeply, whatever makes you calm.

Get moving! Boost your spirits by getting your body in motion.

Laugh—watch a favorite sitcom, cartoon, or movie.

Treat your feet! Pamper your toes with a scrub, lotion, and pretty nail polish.

Here's what makes me feel relaxed and pampered:

Feeling Good

Good health starts on the inside. Write about the things you do that make you **feel happy** and **healthy.**

Battling Bad Habits

If you bite your nails or suck your thumb, you're not alone. The good news is that lots of girls have been able to **break their bad habits** once they put their minds to it. The key to reaching a goal is to **write it down.** The more specific you are about your plan, the more likely you are to **succeed!**

My bad habits:

Choose one bad habit from your list that **you'd like to break.**

Bad habit I'm going to break: ....

....

....

I'll completely break my bad habit by this date: ....

....

....

My daily plan of attack: ....

....

....

....

Here's how I'll reward myself: ....

....

....

....

Hair Hotline

The key to a great "do" is **accepting how your hair is** naturally. And remember, clean and healthy hair is the best look of all! Circle the qualities natural to your hair. Now, underline your dream hair.

Blond

Brunette

Brown

Black

Red

Curly

Smooth

Straight

Short

Thick

Long

Soft

Wavy

Thin

Oily

Shoulder-length

Bouncy

Auburn

Dry

I wish I had my dream hair because

....

....

....

....

The good things about my hair just the way it is:

....

....

....

....

....

....

....

Things I can do with my hair when I need a change:

❑ Clip it   ❑ Put it in a ponytail or pigtails

❑ Braid it   ❑ Tie it back with a scarf

Hair Doodles

A drawing of myself . . .

. . . on a **good hair day**

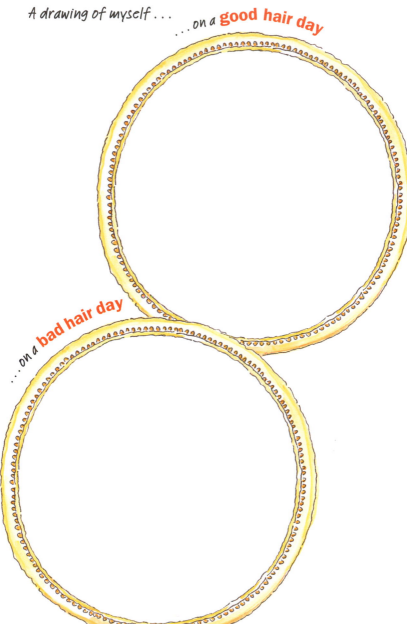

. . . on a **bad hair day**

. . . *with my* **fantasy hairstyle**

. . . *with a* **hairstyle I'm considering**

Serve Yourself!

Just how much from each **food group** should you eat every day? That depends on your age and how physically active you are. The United States Department of Agriculture (USDA) says that a girl who is ten years old and gets 30 to 60 minutes of moderate to vigorous exercise a day should aim to eat this:

Oils:
5 teaspoons daily

Fruits:
1.5 cups daily

Milk/ Dairy:
3 cups daily

Vegetables:
2.5 cups daily

Grains:
6 ounces daily

Meats & Beans:
5 ounces daily

How much from each food group do you eat in a day? Fill in the chart below one day, and add up your results to find out.

	breakfast	+	lunch	+	dinner	+	snacks	=	total
Grains									
Vegetables									
Fruits									
Milk/Dairy									
Meats & Beans									
Oils									

Don't forget **water.** Make sure you drink plenty of it every day, especially during and after exercise.

Healthy Choices

What I should be eating more of:

What I should be eating less of:

I ☐ am ☐ am not drinking enough water.

Five healthy snacks I already like to eat:

1.

2.

3.

4.

5.

If you were doing the grocery shopping for your family, what would be on **your shopping list?**

My Favorite Foods

What I eat for breakfast on school days: ....

....

What I eat for breakfast on weekends: ....

....

My favorite treat: ....

My favorite dinner: ....

When I'm sick, my favorite comfort foods are: ....

....

I like to cook: ....

....

....

I'd like to learn to cook: ....

....

....

Here's a drawing of my favorite birthday cake:

My favorite memory of a dinner is:

If I were a dessert, I would be:

because

My Period

Getting your period. There are probably no other words that will make you feel as excited, scared, or just plain confused. Whether you've already started your period or you're still waiting for it to start, **being prepared will help** you relax.

Keep this in your backpack:

- **One pad or tampon (A makeup bag or an eyeglass case is a good holder.)**

Keep these things at home:

- **A box of pads or tampons**
- **A box of panty liners**
- **A calendar**
- **Medication for cramps (Talk to your mom about getting a pain reliever at the drugstore.)**

It's natural to have lots of **questions** about your period. You'll feel more at ease once you get some answers. Start by pinpointing what's on your mind.

Check any questions that you're **still wondering** about:

❑ How will I know when my period is about to begin?

❑ How will it feel? Will it hurt?

❑ How long will it last?

❑ Will other people know when I have my period?

❑ How do I use a tampon?

❑ How do I know what size pad or tampon to use?

❑ What should I use at night?

❑ Can I exercise or swim when I have my period?

Can We Talk?

The good news is that **you're not alone.** Every teenager or woman has had all the questions you have now. And no question is too silly or too embarrassing to ask. You may feel like crawling into a hole, but remember, getting your period is normal. Find your mom, aunt, or other adult you trust. Muster up your courage and ask, "Do you have time to talk?"

Three adults I feel comfortable talking to about my period and other tricky stuff:

1.

2.

3.

Steps that lead to a **good conversation:**

1. Pick a time when the other person isn't busy. Try bedtime, dinner, or when the two of you are doing something alone together.

2. Start with, "Can we talk?"

3. If you're embarrassed, admit it.

4. Say, "I've been thinking about _____, and I want to ask you a question."

5. Take a deep breath, and ask away.

Here are some questions I'd like to ask:

....

....

....

....

....

....

Writing a note to your mom or other trusted adult
might help if you're just too tongue-tied.

Keeping Track

At first, it can be tricky to predict when your periods will arrive. **Use a calendar,** like the one to the right, to keep track of when they start and end. Put an X in the box of each day you have your period. Once your periods become regular, which usually happens within one to two years, they should last about the same length of time each month.

Don't be surprised if your periods are irregular at first. You might skip a month or two or even have an extra period.

	jan	feb	mar	apr	may	jun	jul	aug	sep	oct	nov	dec
1												
2												
3												
4												
5												
6												
7												
8												
9												
10												
11												
12												
13												
14												
15												
16												
17												
18												
19												
20												
21												
22												
23												
24												
25												
26												
27												
28												
29												
30												
31												

Period Patterns

Once you begin to menstruate regularly, you may notice **patterns** in how you feel physically and emotionally. If you're feeling achy or crabby, this is perfectly normal. **Pay attention** to how you feel, so you can understand your cycle and be prepared.

My period lasts for about .... days. It's heaviest on day # ....

My Body

	Achy	Tired	So-So	Comfortable	Energized
Before period	☐	☐	☐	☐	☐
During	☐	☐	☐	☐	☐
After	☐	☐	☐	☐	☐

My Mood

	Crabby	Sad	So-So	Happy	Psyched
Before period	☐	☐	☐	☐	☐
During	☐	☐	☐	☐	☐
After	☐	☐	☐	☐	☐

Here's how I feel about my period:

Feeling Better

All of the following can make you **feel better** when you have your period. Check which work for you.

☐ Drinking herbal tea

☐ Taking a warm bath

☐ Using a heating pad on my tummy or back

☐ Drinking water

☐ Cutting down on salty foods

☐ Eating fruits and veggies

☐ Taking medication (talk to your mom to see what she recommends)

☐ Exercising

☐ Getting extra sleep

☐ Talking to a friend

☐ Other: ....

☐ Other: ....

☐ Other: ....

Writing down your thoughts can also make you feel better. **Use this page to "talk"** about whatever's on your mind.

Feelings

Feel like you're riding an emotional roller coaster? You're not going crazy, you're just **growing up.** The same hormones that tell your body to wake up and grow can strongly affect your feelings, too. Put an ✗ through all the feelings that **get in the way** of your good mood:

Loneliness

Exhaustion

Anger

Frustration

Embarrassment

Hopelessness

Jealousy

Rage

Selfishness

Stress

Depression

Uncertainty

Boredom

Restlessness

Sadness

Shame

Disappointment

Sulkiness

Meanness

Insecurity

Carelessness

Shyness

Nervousness

Irritability

Guilt

Competitiveness

Impatience

Confusion

Grouchiness

Fear

Disgust

Top three things that make me crabby:

1.

2.

3.

Mood Makeovers

What do you do to **change a bad mood** into a good one?

When I'm sad, I ....

....

....

When I'm lonely, I ....

....

....

When someone has hurt my feelings, I ....

....

....

....

When I'm frustrated, I

 When I'm scared, I

If you feel like you're stuck in a bad mood, let a grown-up know. It is never silly to ask for help.

How I'm Feeling

Time out! **How do you feel** about all these changes? What are you thinking about your body right now? Use this space to pour out what's on your mind:

Heart-to-Heart

Start a conversation with a woman you know. Maybe she's your mom, your aunt, or a neighbor. Find out how things have changed or stayed the same since she was your age. Your list of questions might include:

What was your favorite subject in school? What subject was difficult for you?

Did you have a crush on a boy? Who was he, and what did you like about him?

What sports, hobbies, or clubs were you involved in?

Did you have a best friend when you were my age? What did the two of you do together? Did you ever have a fight? Where is she now?

Who was your favorite teacher? Why?

What did you want to be when you grew up?

How old were you when you got your period, and how did you feel about it?

What famous people did you admire? Did you hang their pictures up in your room?

Did you ever get lonely? What would you do to make yourself feel better?

How did your family celebrate the holidays? Was there a present you wished for? What special present did you give?

Do you remember a time you were really scared?

What birthday do you most remember? How did you celebrate?

How are things for me different from or the same as when you were growing up?

Words of Wisdom

When you have a **heart-to-heart talk,** chances are you'll learn something new. Jotting down the information is a good way to remember it. Use these two pages to **record your conversation.**

Get Moving!

Remember that your body is a work in progress. Try not to focus on what it looks like. Your body is in the process of big changes. Instead, think about all the **great things your body can do.** Start by circling all the things below that you can do:

Whistle

Wiggle my toes in the sand

Balance

Tap a beat

Jump

Swim

Draw

Do a handstand

Rollerblade

Hug

Ride a bike

Run

Ice-skate

Dance

Catch fireflies

Jump rope

Do a cartwheel

Climb

Skip

Play badminton

Go sledding

Give a piggyback ride

Play Ping-Pong

Dive

Skateboard

Chase butterflies

Play hide-and-seek

Snowboard

Laugh

Build a snow fort

Take a bow

Walk my dog

Hit a tennis ball

Do a somersault

Play kickball

Walk barefoot

Sing

Hike

Bake cookies

Catch a Frisbee

Play an instrument

Ski

Kick a soccer ball

Serve a volleyball

Throw a football

Ready? Set? Go!

Are you a couch potato or a jumping bean? Take this **quiz** to find out where you fall on our Move-o-Meter! Circle the letter next to the answer that describes you best.

1. You're finally out of the car. You've slapped on some sunscreen and you're ready to hit the beach. The first thing you do is . . .

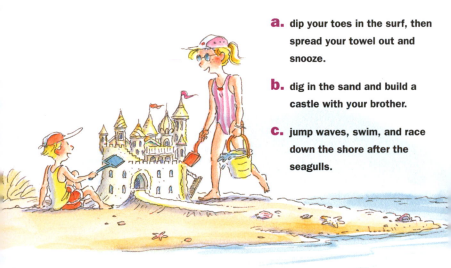

a. dip your toes in the surf, then spread your towel out and snooze.

b. dig in the sand and build a castle with your brother.

c. jump waves, swim, and race down the shore after the seagulls.

2. You have 105 TV channels, but today they're all showing reruns. You . . .

a. watch your six favorite shows again to catch anything you missed seeing the first time.

b. watch a video, then go outside to practice shooting free throws.

c. watch TV? Who has time?

3. Your best friend is sleeping over on Friday! You can't wait to . . .

    a. play video games until the sun comes up.

    b. gather everything you need to make tons of bracelets to sell to your friends.

    c. turn on your favorite songs and dance the night away.

4. Good news: a neighborhood friend invited you over. Bad news: your dad can't drive you. You decide to . . .

    a. stay home. No ride? No way! You talk on the phone with your friend instead.

    b. walk over and meet your friend at the park—it's halfway.

    c. hop on your bike and pedal to your friend's house.

5. What a great day you've had camping with your family! Now comes the best part—sitting around the campfire. You volunteer to . . .

    a. break up the graham crackers to make s'mores.

    b. walk around the campsite to find perfect marshmallow sticks for everyone.

    c. scour the forest to gather armfuls of wood.

6. It's Saturday afternoon, and the rain outside means you're staying inside. You decide to . . .

    a. cuddle up with a blanket and read a book from cover to cover.

    b. grab your watercolors and paint a picture for a friend.

    c. rearrange your entire room from top to bottom.

7. Your mom says she wants to do something together, just the two of you. Best of all, you get to pick the activity. You choose . . .

    a. a night on the couch watching family videos of you as a baby.

    b. an afternoon of making a scrapbook filled with your silliest vacation photos.

    c. a day of swimming at the pool. This time you know Mom will go off the high dive, too!

8. At summer camp, you'd be voted . . .

    a. Bed Bug.

    b. Craft Queen.

    c. Game Girl.

Answers

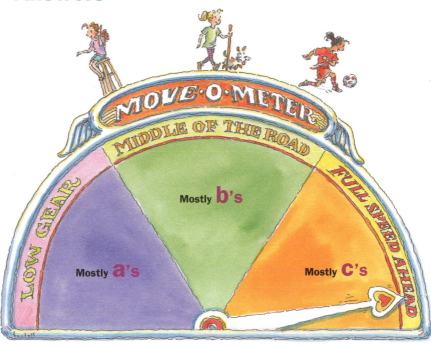

MOVE·O·METER

MIDDLE OF THE ROAD

Mostly **b's**

LOW GEAR

Mostly **a's**

FULL SPEED AHEAD

Mostly **c's**

If you circled mostly **a's,** you're a girl who knows how to relax. But remember to flex your muscles and work up a sweat for 20 minutes three times a week or more to keep your body healthy and strong. Find something active that you like to do—then do it! Not into competition? Try a dance class, in-line skating, or swimming to get your heart pounding.

If you circled mostly **b's,** you're a creative girl with lots of ideas. Use your imagination to find ways to get moving! Play volleyball with friends, start a car-washing business in your neighborhood, or walk through the woods to collect stuff to make a craft. You might also try activities like martial arts or yoga to challenge your body and your brain!

If you circled mostly **c's,** you're a mover and a shaker. You love to be active, and your muscles love it, too! Keep going, and invite a friend—or even Mom or Dad—to go with you!

Go Play!

Yes, exercise is important. But it's also fun! Whether you like team sports or solo workouts, **getting active** is good for you.

I play ....

....

I also like to ....

....

I prefer: ☐ team sports ☐ going solo

My favorite time of day to exercise is ....

because ....

....

....

When my heart's pumping, I feel ....

....

....

....

....

After I'm done, I feel

Other ways I get my body moving are

I feel strongest when I

A sport or activity I'd like to learn is

Having Fun

Describe the last time you **worked up a sweat** and **had fun,** too.

What's your favorite way to spend a
Saturday afternoon?

Getting My ZZZ's

Get the most out of your day by recharging your body at night. Most girls need at least eight hours of sleep each night. Keeping a **bedtime routine** helps your body wind down and prepare to rest.

My bedtime on weekdays: .... weekends: ....

Time I begin getting ready for bed: ....

Things I do right before bedtime: ....

....

Hours of sleep I get each night on weekdays: ....

Hours of sleep I get each night on weekends: ....

I sleep with: ☐ my bedroom light on

☐ a night-light on

☐ the lights off

I keep my: ☐ door closed

☐ door open

☐ door ajar

A drawing of . . .

. . . my **favorite pajamas**

. . . my **favorite pillowcase**

Nightmares

Describe a dream you hope never to have again.

....

....

....

....

....

....

....

....

....

....

....

....

....

Sweet Dreams

Describe a dream you'd like
to have again.

....

....

....

....

....

....

....

....

....

....

....

....

....

....

Imagine

The secret to a good night's sleep is to **unwind your mind.** Create a nighttime version of a daydream. Think of your brain as your own personal television. You are the star and the director. Close your eyes and imagine yourself in a place that makes you happy and calm, doing something that is relaxing.

In my vision, here's . . .

where I am:

what I'm doing:

what I hear:

what I feel:

what I smell:

whom I'm with:

What I'm Thankful For

Ever tried counting sheep to fall asleep? Boring, huh? Try this instead: **count all the things you're thankful for**—include the little things, too. The list will quiet your worries in a hurry.

What's On My Mind

Sometimes our problems are all we can think about. Getting those thoughts out of your head and onto paper will help. Think of this as space to **unload what's weighing on your mind.**

Here's what's bugging me:

Here's what I'm worried about:

Think Positive

Now, shift your focus. Think about the **things that make you feel good.**

Here's what I'm excited about: ....

....

....

....

....

....

....

....

....

....

....

....

Here's what I'm looking forward to:

Stay in Control

When you're angry, it's easy for your emotions to take over your actions. But slamming a door, yelling, or sulking will only make matters worse. **Talking things over** is the only solution. That means expressing yourself calmly—and *listening,* too.

Think about the last time you were really angry with someone.

What happened that made you angry?

Did you talk to the person who made you angry?

If so, how did you feel about the conversation? Did it go well or was

it rocky?

Do you think the other person listened to you?

Did you listen to her?

How do you think the other person felt about the conversation?

Do you wish you could go back and start the conversation over? If so,

what would you do differently?

If you kept your feelings to yourself, what happened?

Time Out!

When your temper heats up—stop! **Take a break** and cool down before you talk about your feelings. Otherwise, you might say something you'll regret. Once you're calm, you're ready to have a good conversation.

Check off the ways you blow off steam:

❑ Write in my journal

❑ Take a walk

❑ Play with my pet

❑ Ride my bike

❑ Read a book

❑ Take a bath

❑ Talk to a friend

❑ Take a deep breath and count to 10, 20, or 100—whatever it takes!

❑ Other

Three steps to expressing how you feel:

1. Describe exactly what made you angry.

2. Tell how it made you feel.

3. Try to agree on a way to handle things in the future.

Sometimes talking about feelings brings people closer together. Has this ever happened to you? Describe a time when talking things over not only ended an argument, but also made your friendship even stronger.

You're the Expert!

You have experience handling life's twists and turns, so don't be surprised by how much you already know. Pretend you're the writer of an advice column, and **answer the following letters.**

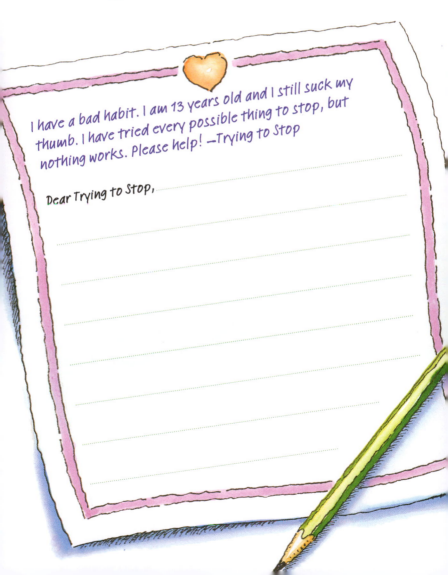

I have a bad habit. I am 13 years old and I still suck my thumb. I have tried every possible thing to stop, but nothing works. Please help! —Trying to Stop

Dear Trying to Stop,

I'm nine years old, and I just got glasses. I need them to see the chalkboard in class. I am afraid people will laugh at me and call me names. But I like my glasses. What should I do?
—Christy

Dear Christy,

You're the Expert!

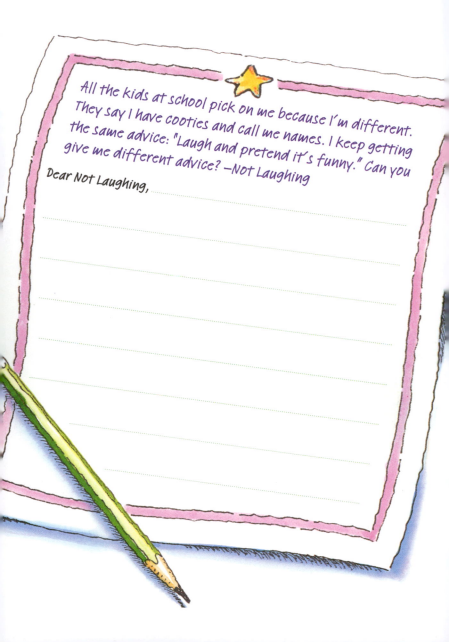

All the kids at school pick on me because I'm different. They say I have cooties and call me names. I keep getting the same advice: "Laugh and pretend it's funny." Can you give me different advice? —Not Laughing

Dear Not Laughing,

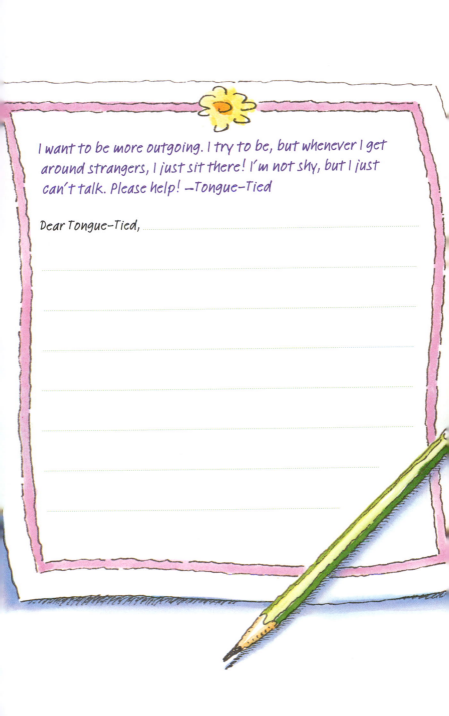

I want to be more outgoing. I try to be, but whenever I get around strangers, I just sit there! I'm not shy, but I just can't talk. Please help! —Tongue-Tied

Dear Tongue-Tied,

Dear Me,

Giving others advice is sometimes easier than helping our-selves. But you can be your own best friend, too. When you have a problem, **write it down.** This will help you pinpoint what's bothering you.

Here's my problem:

Now, step away, and pretend the problem belongs to a friend who's seeking your advice. What would you tell her?

Dear friend, Here's my advice:

Sincerely,

Picture Perfect

Look how far you've come, and imagine where you're going!

A drawing or photo of . . .

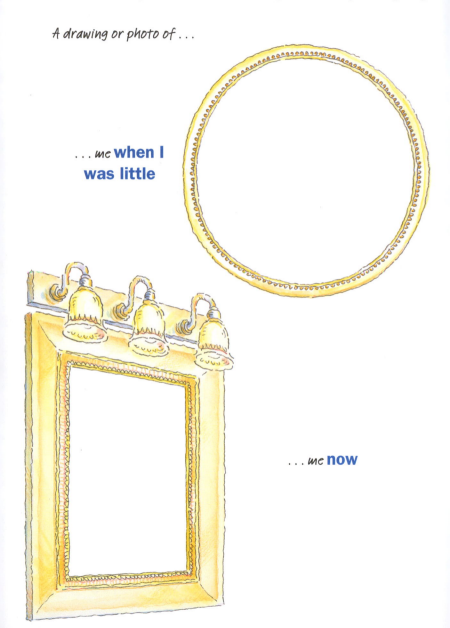

. . . *me* **when I was little**

. . . *me* **now**

What I might be doing:

....

....

....

....

....

Where I might live:

....

....

....

....

....

A drawing or clipping of how I imagine
I'll look **when I grow up**

Make Wishes

Wishes become goals when you put them on paper. Write your wishes upon these stars, and you'll be one step **closer to making them come true!**